GREAT
CARD
GAMES

GREAT CARD GAMES

Alfred Sheinwold,
Sheila Anne Barry, and
Margie Golick

Main Street
A division of Sterling Publishing Co., Inc.
New York

10 9 8 7 6 5 4 3 2 1

Published by Sterling Publishing Co., Inc.
387 Park Avenue South, New York, NY 10016

© 2005 by Sterling Publishing Co., Inc.

This book is comprised of material from
the following Sterling Publishing Co., Inc. titles:
The Little Giant® Book of Card Games © 2003
by Sterling Publishing Co., Inc.
101 Best Family Card Games © 1992 by Sterling Publishing Co., Inc.

Design by StarGraphics Studio

Printed in China
All rights reserved

Sterling ISBN 1-4027-3136-1

For information about custom editions, special sales, premium and
corporate purchases, please contact Sterling Special Sales
Department at 800-805-5489 or specialsales@sterlingpub.com.

Table of Contents

GREAT CARD GAMES

Authors

OF PLAYERS: 2–5

This game is a lot like "Go Fish," but it can be played with great skill.

The Object of the Game

To win more books (4 cards of the same rank) than any other player.

The Deal

Deal out all 52 cards, even though they may not come out even.

The Play

At your turn, you ask for a single card naming both its rank and its suit. For example, you might say, "Bill, give me the Jack of Spades." Your turn continues if you get the card you asked for, but it passes to the left as soon as you ask for a card that the player doesn't have.

You can buy decks of cards that are specially made for playing "Authors," so that you can ask a player for William Shakespeare or Ernest Hemingway. But it's just as much fun to play "Authors" with a regular deck of cards.

Basic Rummy

OF PLAYERS: 2–6

The Object of the Game

To win points from your opponents. To do this, you have to match up your cards by getting three or four of a kind, or sequences of cards that are next to each other in rank and the same in suit.

For example, you could match up three Kings or four 10s, or a sequence of cards like:

Highest · *Lowest*

or

A typical sequence

Another typical sequence

You need at least three cards for a sequence.

The Deal

Deal ten cards to each player when two are playing; seven cards to each when three or four are playing, and six cards to each person when five or six are playing.

Put the rest of the cards facedown in the middle of the table, forming the stock. Turn the top card faceup, starting the discard pile.

The Play

Each player at the table plays in turn, beginning with the player to the dealer's left. In your turn, you do three things:

You draw a card from the stock.

You meld, if you can.

You discard.

When you draw, you may pick up the top card of the stock or the top card of the discard pile. You add this card to your hand.

To meld, you put a group of matched cards down on the table, if you are lucky enough to have three or four of a kind or of a sequence.

You don't have to put them down, though. You can keep them in your hand, if you want.

You can also, on your turn, add to any meld that is out on the table.

For example, if someone has put down three Kings, you may add the fourth King when it is your turn to play. If someone has put down the 6, 7, and 8 of Diamonds, you could add the 9 and 10 of Diamonds, or the 5 and 4, or any such card or group of cards.

After you have drawn and melded—or after you have declined to meld—it is your turn to discard. You can take any card from your hand and put it on top of the faceup pile in the middle of the table. This completes your turn.

If, on your turn, you manage to meld all your cards, you win the game. You must begin your play with a draw, thus adding one card to your hand, and then you must meld either all the cards in your hand, or all but one, which would be your discard.

If no player has melded all his cards (called "going out") by the time the stock is used up, the next player may take either the top card of the discard pile or the top card of the new stock that has been formed by turning the discard pile over. In either case, the game goes on as before, until somebody does go out.

Scoring

The winner of a hand scores points by counting up the hands of all the other players in the game. Each loser counts the cards in his hand according to the following scale:

Point Value of the Cards

Picture cards = 10 points each
Aces = 1 point each
Other cards = face value

A loser does not count cards that he has previously melded on the table, but he does count any cards that remain in his hand—*whether or not these cards match!*

When you meld all your cards in one turn, without previously melding or adding to anybody else's meld, it is called "going Rummy." Whenever you "go Rummy," you win double the normal amount from each of the other players.

Keep score with pencil and paper, setting up a column for each player. Whenever a player wins a hand, put the amounts that he wins from the other players into his winning column.

Some players agree on a stopping time when they play "Rummy." The winner is the player with the highest score when that time is up. Other players end a game when any player reaches a certain total score, such as 500 points. The score for each player is added up at the end of each hand.

Strategy

In all games of the Rummy family, you try to build up your hand by keeping cards that match and discarding cards that don't.

For example, if you drew the 10 of Spades, you would tend to keep it if your hand contained one or more 10s, or the Jack of Spades or the 9 of Spades. Even if it did not immediately give you a meld, it would probably bring you closer to one.

If you drew a card that didn't match anything in your hand, you would either discard it immediately, or wait for a later chance to discard it.

If the player to your left picks up a card from the discard pile, this gives you a clue to what's in his hand. If, for example, he picks up the 9 of Diamonds, you know that he must have other 9s or other Diamonds in the neighborhood of the 9. If convenient, you might avoid throwing another 9 or another Diamond in that vicinity onto the discard pile.

This is called "playing defensively." You don't need to bother with defensive play against anybody but the player to your left, since your discard would be covered up by the time any other player wanted to draw.

The advantage of melding is that you cannot lose the value of those cards, even if some other player wins the hand.

The advantage of holding a meld in your hand is that nobody can add to the meld while it is still in your hand. A second advantage is the possibility of going "Rummy" all in one play.

It sometimes pays to hold up a meld, but most successful Rummy players make it a habit to put melds down fairly quickly. It's usually safe to hold up a meld for one to two turns, but after that it's dangerous. If another player goes out before you have melded, you will lose those matched cards just as though they were unmatched.

Blackjack
OF PLAYERS: 3 or more

Card Values
Ace: one or eleven points
King, Queen, Jack: ten points
Other cards: face value
(The highest combination is an Ace and a black Jack).

The Object of the Game
To have cards that add up to twenty-one, or come very close without going over.

The Deal
Each player receives one card placed facedown and one card placed face-up.

The Play
Each player looks at his or her facedown card and makes an "ante," or token bet, into the pot. (You can use coins or any other type of counters). The player sitting to the left of the dealer now has two choices:

Stick: To "stick" means to not take any more cards.
Hit: To "hit" (the player says "Hit me") means to get another face-up card from the dealer. This can be

repeated as many times as the player would like, but if the total of the face-up cards becomes more than twenty-one, the player must say "Bust" and has lost.

Play continues around clockwise, with each player getting a chance to "stick" or "hit." After everyone has "Busted" or decided to "Stick," the player with the cards closest to twenty-one without going over wins the pot.

Tip

Most people decide to "stick" when the value of their cards reaches eighteen because there are very few cards that you can get and still stay under twenty-one.

Canfield
OF PLAYERS: 1

"Canfield" is one of the most popular solitaire games in the world. A shorter, faster game than the equally popular "Klondike" (page 39), "Canfield" is played much the same way, but it starts from a different basic layout.

"Canfield" got its name in an interesting way. Mr. Canfield owned a gambling house in Saratoga Springs in the 1890s. He used to sell his customers packs of cards at $50 each, and then pay them back $5 for every card they were able to score. The average number of cards you could expect to score in a game was five or six, so Mr. Canfield did pretty well.

The Layout

Count out 13 cards into one pile and put it in front of you faceup and a little to your left. Then put a 14th card to the right of the pile, and slightly above it. Whatever that card is, it becomes the foundation card of this particular game. As the other cards of the same rank appear, you'll be placing them too in the foundation row.

Next you lay out a row of four cards below the foundation card, faceup.

The Object of the Game
To build the foundation cards into four complete suits of 13 cards each.

The Play
No cards are ever built on the 13-pile. The object is to unload it.

For example, in the illustration above, you couldn't put a 5—or any other card—on the 6.

Cards from the 13 pile can be played only onto the foundations or into the four card row when a space opens up.

First check the four-card spread carefully to see whether you can make any moves. Besides playing cards to the foundations, you can build cards onto the four-card row, one by one moving downwards, in alternating colors—first red, then black, then red, and so on.

For instance, in the diagram on page 231, the 3 of Hearts can go onto the 4 of Spades, the 7 of Diamonds can go up into the foundation row, and the 6 of Spades can come down from the 13-pile into the row of four. Once it does, you can play the 5 of Hearts onto it.

You are permitted to move sequences of cards as one unit.

For example, the 3 and 4 may be moved together onto the 5 and 6, so your layout would look like the one on page 233.

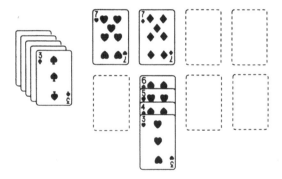

Then you can fill the other open spaces in the four-card row with cards from the 13-pile.

Now start turning up cards from the pack in batches of three, playing them either to the foundations, to the four-card row, or to the wastepile. You can always play the top card of the wastepile.

When the cards from the 13 card pile are gone, you can fill spaces in the four-card row with cards from your hand or from the wastepile. Re-deal as many times as you want.

Casino

OF PLAYERS: 2-4

This game is best with two players.

The Object of the Game
To win the highest number of points. You get points by capturing the most cards, the most Spades, Aces, the 10 of Diamonds (Big Casino), and the 2 of Spades (Little Casino).

The Deal
The deck of 52 cards is used up in six deals. In the first deal:
- The non-dealer receives two cards facedown.
- Then two cards are put faceup on the table.
- Then the dealer gives himself two cards facedown.

And the process repeats, so that each player and the table have four cards each.

In the remaining five deals, the dealer continues to give each player four cards—two at a time—but does not give any additional cards to the table.

The Play
Beginning with the non-dealer, each player in turn must play one card from his hand, until all four of his cards are gone. If he can find no better use for it, he simply places his card faceup on the table. This is called trailing. Whenever he can, though, he uses his card to capture cards from the table.

Pairing
You may win cards in various ways. The simplest way is by

pairing. You may capture a card on the table with another of the same rank from your hand—a 5 with a 5, a Jack with a Jack, and so on.

With a picture card—a Jack, Queen, or King—you may capture only one card, but with a card of lower rank, you may take two or three of the same kind at the same time. If there are two 7s on the table and you have a 7 in your hand, for example, you can take all three.

Each player keeps captured cards in a pile, facedown.

Building

All the lower cards—Ace to 10—may be captured by building. Ace counts as 1. Each other card counts as its own value. Cards on the table may be taken in by higher cards to equal their sum.

For example, you may take a 5 and a 2 with a 7. You may take an Ace and a 9 with a 10. You may, at the same time, take additional cards by pairing. Suppose that the cards on the table are 9, 8, 5, 4, and Ace. You could take them all with a single 9, since the 9s pair up, 8 and 1 make 9, and 5 and 4 make 9.

Leaving a Build

Suppose that you have 8 and 3 in your hand, and there is a 5 on the table. You may put the 3 on the 5 and say, "Building 8." Your intention is to capture the build with your 8 on your next turn, because you are allowed to play only one card from your hand at a time.

If your opponent has an 8, she can capture your build. That's the risk of leaving a build. Yet the risk is usually worth taking, because in building, you make it harder for your opponent to capture cards. She cannot take the 5 or the 3 by pairing or by making a build of her own.

Of course, you may not leave a build unless you have a card in your hand that can take it. You are, however, allowed to duplicate your build before taking it in. Suppose you have two 8s in your hand. After building the 5 and 3, you could on your next turn simply put one 8 on the build, and take it with the other 8 on your third turn.

Or suppose—after you build the 5 and 3, your opponent trails a 6, and you have a 2 in your hand (besides the 8), You may take your 2 and put it, along with the 6, on the 5-3 build, and wait until your next turn to take in the duplicated build.

An important rule is that when you have left a build on the table, you must deal with it at your next turn—take it in—or increase or duplicate it. You are not allowed to trail or to take in other cards instead.

Increasing a Build

Suppose that your opponent has laid a 4 from her hand on a 5 on the table, and called out, "Building 9." You have an Ace and a 10. You may add the Ace to her build and say "Building 10." You are allowed to increase a build of your own in the same way.

But there are two restrictions on increasing a build. First, you may increase only a single build, such as the 5-4—not one that has been duplicated in any way—such as 5-4-9. Second, the card you use to increase it must come from your hand, not from the table.

Scoring

After the last card of the sixth deal is played, any cards remaining on the table go to the player who was last to capture cards. Then each player looks through his captured cards and counts up his score, as follows:

Cards: for winning 27 or more cards   3 points
Spades: for winning 7or more Spades   1 point
Big Casino: the 10 of Diamonds   2 points
Little Casino: the 2 of Spades   1 point
Aces: each counting 1   4 points
   Total of   **11 points**

The first one to reach a total of 21 or more points wins.

Cheat (I Doubt It)
OF PLAYERS: 3 or more

When you have three or four players, use one deck of cards. When you are playing with five or more, shuffle two packs together.

The Object of the Game
To get rid of all your cards.

The Deal
Two or three cards at a time are dealt so that each player gets an equal number of cards. When only a few cards are left, deal one at a time as far as the cards will go.

The Play
The player to the dealer's left puts from one to four cards facedown in the middle of the table, announcing that she is putting down that number of Aces.

The next player puts down one to four cards and announces that he is putting down that number of 2s.

The next player in turn does the same thing, stating that he is putting down that number of 3s. And the play proceeds in this sequence:

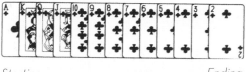

Starting   *Ending*

When any player puts down cards and makes his announcement, any other player may say, "I doubt it." The suspect cards must immediately be turned faceup. If the statement was true, the doubter must take the entire pile into his hand. If the statement was false, the player who made the false statement must take the pile.

When you're using two packs shuffled together, a player may put down any number of cards, from one to eight.

When a player puts his last cards n the table, some other player must say, "I doubt it," since otherwise the game ends automatically. If the statement turns out to be true, the player wins the game.

A player who has no cards at all of the kind that she is supposed to put down is not allowed to skip her turn. She must put down one or more cards anyway and try to get away with her untruthful announcement. If somebody doubts her claim, she will have to pick up the pile.

If two or more people say, "I doubt it," at the same time, the one nearest the player's left wins the tie and must pick up the pile, if the statement turns out to be true after all.

Clover Leaf

OF PLAYERS: 1

This is one of the most delightful solitaire games, but you need a lot of space for it..

The Layout
Lay out the whole deck in sets of three, faceup, like this:

One single card will be left over, which becomes a set of its own.

The only cards that may be moved are the exposed ones on top of the sets. They are built up on the foundation or on the top cards of other sets by suit, building downwards.

The Object of the Game
To release the Aces and build them up in suit to Kings.

The Play
Once you have the cards laid out, move the Aces that are available onto the foundations.

For example, in the layout on page 240, the Ace of Hearts can go on one of the foundations, so can the 2 and 3 of Hearts. Then the 3 of Spades can go onto the 4 of Spades, and so on.

Continue to build on the top cards of the three-leaf clovers, one card at a time. When a clover is entirely eliminated, it is not replaced.

Re-deals

You get two. To re-deal, gather up the clovers that are left, shuffle the cards, and set them down in groups of three as before. Any leftover cards are sets by themselves.

Special Bonus

In the last re-deal, when you're stuck, you get one free move—one card you can pull from underneath one or two others, and play in any way you want.

Concentration
OF PLAYERS: any number

The Object of the Game
To capture the largest number of cards.

The Deal
Spread the cards facedown on a table. Don't bother to put them down neatly, but just jumble them up, making sure that no two cards overlap.

The Play
Before they begin, the players need to know what their turn is, whether they are first, second, third, and so on.

The first player turns up any card and then turns up any other card. If the two cards match (for example, if they are two Aces or two Kings), the first player captures them as her pair. She then gets another turn, and proceeds to turn up two more cards in the hope of finding a pair. When she turns up two cards that are not a pair, she must turn them facedown again in the same position. It now becomes the turn of the next player.

Crazy Eights
OF PLAYERS: 2–8

This game is best for two, three, or four players. In a four-handed game, the players who sit across the table from each other are partners.

The Object of the Game

To get rid of all your cards. The first player to get rid of them wins.

The Deal

Deal out seven cards to each player in a two-handed game, five to each player when more than two are playing.

Put the rest of the cards on the table facedown as the stock. Turn the top card faceup to begin another pile.

The Play

The player to the left of the dealer must match the card that has been turned up. That means he must put down a card of the same suit or of the same rank.

For example, suppose that the card first turned up is the 9 of Spades. The first player needs to put down another Spade or a 9. That card is placed on top of the turned-up card. It is up to the next player to match the new card either in suit or in rank.

The four 8s are wild, which means that you may play an 8 at any time when it is your turn. When putting down an 8, you are allowed to call it any suit at all, as you please.

For example, you might put down the 8 of Hearts and say "Spade." The next player would then have to follow with a Spade.

If, at your turn, you cannot play, you must draw cards from the top of the stock until you are able to play or until there are no more cards left. You are allowed to draw cards from the stock at your turn, even if you are able to play without drawing. This is sometimes a good idea.

Sometimes a hand ends in a block, with nobody able to play, and with nobody having played out. The hand is then won by the player with the smallest number of cards. If two or more players tie for this honor, the hand is declared a tie.

Strategy

The most important principle is not to play an 8 too quickly. If you waste an 8 when you are not really in trouble, you won't have it to save you when the going gets tough.

The time that you really need an 8 to protect yourself is when you have been run out of a suit.

For example, after several Spades have been played, you might not be able to get another Spade, even if you drew every single card in the stock.

If you are also unable to match the rank of the card that has been put down, you may be forced to pick up the entire stock before your turn is over. From here on, of course, it will be very hard for you to avoid a disastrous defeat. An 8 will save you from this kind of misfortune, since you can put it down in place of a Spade, and you may be able to call a suit that does for your opponent what the Spade would have done for you.

If you're lucky, you won't have to play the 8 as your next to last card. It would be better to play it when your next turn comes—and win the hand. To play an 8 with more than two cards in your hand is seldom wise. It is usually a good idea to draw a few cards from stock in order to find a playable card.

Tip

The best way to beat an opponent is to run her out of some suit. If you have several cards in one suit, chances are your opponent will not have so many. As often as you get the chance, keep coming back to your long suit, until your opponent is unable to match your card. Eventually, she will have to draw from stock and may have to load herself up badly before she is able to play.

Forty Thieves
OF PLAYERS: 1

You need two decks of cards.

The Layout
Deal four rows of ten cards each, overlapping, as in the picture. Aces, as they become available, are moved up above the layout as foundations.

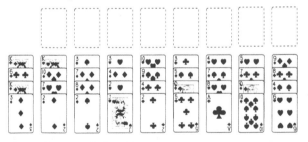

The Object of the Game
Build all eight Aces to Kings in suit.

The Play
First, build what you can to the foundations. Then build on the layout itself, downward in suit.

For example, in the illustration on page 295, the Ace of Clubs can be played up to the foundation row. So can the 2. The 2 of Diamonds can be placed on the 3 of Diamonds.

When you have exhausted all the possibilities, start going through the cards one by one, building onto the foundations or layout or discarding the unplayable cards into a wastepile. The top card of that wastepile is available too.

When a space opens up in the layout, you can fill it with any card — one from the layout, the top card from the wastepile, or a card from your hand.

Frog

OF PLAYERS: 1

Play this game with two decks of cards. Another name for it is "Toad in the Hole."

The Layout

Count out 13 cards and place them in one pile faceup. Make sure no Aces are in the pile. If there are, replace them with other cards. Then place one Ace next to the pack as a foundation. As other Aces turn up, place them next to it.

Object of the Game
Build all the Aces up by suit to Kings.

The Play
Go through the stockpile card by card. When cards are not playable, place them in a row of their own underneath the foundation row. Set up a row of five piles that you will have available for this purpose. You can put the cards in any positions you choose—all in one pile, if you want.

Gimme

The Object of the Game
To be first to get rid of all the cards in your hand.

The Deal
You need two decks of cards—with jokers—shuffled together. If you have seven or more players, use three decks of cards.

   Deal eleven cards to each player. The dealer puts the rest of the pack in the center of the table and turns the top card faceup. Each game consists of seven hands; each one begins in the same way. The player to the dealer's left may take that card. If she doesn't want it, any player who does may say "Gimme." The one closest to the dealer gets it, but he must take the top facedown card along with it.

The Play
Each player in turn picks a card from the top of the deck

and discards one into a separate discard pile faceup beside the deck. The player to his left may pick up the discard, but if he does not, other players may say "Gimme" and the game goes on as above.

You are allowed only three "Gimme's" in any hand (which means you may get a maximum of 17 cards). At your turn, you may meld cards according to the following rules:

First hand: Two sets
Second Hand: One set, one sequence
Third Hand: Two sequences
Fourth Hand: Three sets
Fifth Hand: Two sets, one sequence
Sixth Hand: Two runs, one sequence
Seventh Hand: Three runs

The sets and sequences for each hand do not have to be laid down at the same time.

Jokers are wild and may substitute for any card in a sequence or a set.

At your turn, you may also put down cards that add onto the melds already on the table.

For example, if there is a set of sevens on the table, you can meld a 7 from your own hand. If there is a run of Hearts from the 2 to the 5, you could meld an Ace of Hearts or a 6 from your hand.

A hand ends as soon as one player has no more cards. Other players total the value of all the cards left in their hands. These count against them.

Point Value of the Cards

Joker = 50 points
Ace = 25 points

Jack, Queen, King = 10 points each
All other cards = 5 points

The winner is the player with the lowest score after all seven hands have been played.

Gin Rummy
OF PLAYERS: 2

The Object of the Game

To reduce the count of your unmatched cards. A matched set in "Gin" is the same as a "meld" in "Basic Rummy": three or four cards of the same rank, or in sequence in the same suit: For example, here are two matched sets:

In "Gin," Aces rank low:

Highest   *Lowest*

This is a sequence.   *This is not.*

Point Value of the Cards

Ace = 1
Picture cards = 10
Other cards = face value

The Deal

Each player gets ten cards, dealt one at a time. Place the rest of the deck facedown in the middle of the table to form the stock. Turn over the top card of the stock beside it. This upcard starts the discard pile.

The Play

The non-dealer plays first. If she wants the upcard she may take it, but if she doesn't, she must say so without drawing. Then the dealer may take it if he wants, and discard one card from his hand, faceup. After he has taken or refused it, the non-dealer continues with her turn, drawing one card—the top card of the stock or the card that the dealer has just discarded. Then she discards one card faceup on the discard pile and the play continues with no further complications.

Knocking

All melding is kept in the hand until some player brings matters to a halt by laying down all his ten cards, either by "ginning" or "knocking."

To gin, you lay down all your cards in melds. When you knock, you have unmatched cards whose total is ten or less. You may knock only when it is your turn to play, after drawing and before discarding. The final discard is made facedown, indicating the intention to knock. If you simply placed the card faceup, you could be stopped, because—according to the rules—the faceup discard would end your turn.

As you play, you arrange your cards in matched sets with the unmatched cards to one side. It is customary to announce the total count or your unmatched cards by saying something like, "Knocking with five." Your opponent then shows her hand. She is entitled to lay off cards on your sets, provided that you don't have a gin hand—all ten cards—matched.

For example, if you had this hand:

Knock Hand

your opponent could lay off the fourth Jack and the 10 and 6 of Hearts, if she had any of those cards.

Scoring

Your opponent counts her remaining unmatched cards after laying off what she can onto your hand. If the count is higher than yours, you win the difference. If your opponent has the same count that you have—or a lower one—she scores the difference, if any, plus 25 points for undercutting you.

If you lay down a gin hand, your opponent may not lay off any cards on it. You win your opponent's count plus a bonus of 25 points. You can't win that bonus if you knock.

Keeping Score

Keep score with pencil and paper. Enter the result of hand in the column under the winner's name. Draw a line below the item and then write the running total. The lines between the items are important, to keep track of how many hands were won by each player. Each player is credited with 25 points for each winning hand. This is called the "line" or "box score."

If you are the first player to reach a total of 100 or more, you win the game and score a bonus of 100 points.

If your opponent has not scored a single point, that is a "shutout"— or a "whitewash," "skunk," "Schneider," "goose egg," etc., and you get an additional 100 points for that.

Go Boom

 # OF PLAYERS: 2 or more

The Object of the Game
To get rid of all your cards.

The Deal
Deal seven cards to each player. Put the rest of the pack facedown in the middle of the table.

The Play
The player to the left of the dealer puts any card on the table. The next player to her left must follow by matching the suit or rank of that card. Each player in turn after this must match the previous card in suit or rank.

For example, suppose the first player puts down the Jack of Diamonds. The next player may follow with any Diamond or with another Jack. If the second player decides to follow with the Jack of Clubs, the third player may then match with a Club or with one of the two remaining Jacks.

When a player cannot match the previous card, he must draw cards from the stock until he is able to play. If a player uses up the stock without finding a playable card, he may say "Pass," and his turn passes to the next player.

When everybody at the table has had the chance to play or say "Pass," the cards are examined to see who has played the highest card.

The cards rank as follows:

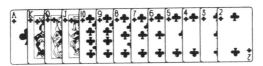

Highest   *Lowest*

The player who put down the highest card has the right to begin the next play. If there is a tie for first place among cards of the same rank, the card that was played first is considered higher.

The play continues until one player gets rid of all his cards and wins the hand.

If you want to use a system of point scoring, have each loser count the cards left in his hand as follows:

Each picture card = 10
Each Ace = 1
Each other card = its face value

The winner of the hand is credited with the total of all points lost by the other players.

Strategy
The strategy in "Go Boom" is much the same as in "Crazy Eights." You try to run your opponent out of a suit in

hopes that he will not be able to match your play with a card of the same suit or the same rank.

In the early stages of play it is useful to put down as high a card as possible in order to have the best chance to win the privilege of beginning the next play.

Go Fish
OF PLAYERS: 3–5

The Object of the Game

To form more "books" than any other player. A book in this game is four of a kind, such as four Kings, four Queens, and so on.

The Deal

If only two play, deal seven cards to each. If four or five play, deal five cards to each. Put the rest of the pack face-down on the table, forming the stock.

The Play

The player to the dealer's left begins. Let's say that's you. You say to some other player, "Jane, give me your 9s." You must mention the name of the player you are speaking to (Jane), and you must mention the exact rank that you want (9s), and you must have at least one card of the rank that you are asking for (9) in your hand.

The player you are speaking to (Jane), must hand over all the 9s she has in her hand, but if she has none, she says, "Go Fish."

Then you draw the top card of the stock. The turn to ask then passes to the player to your left.

If you succeed in getting some cards when you ask for them, you keep your turn and may ask again. You may ask the same player or some different player, and you may ask for any rank in your new question.

If you have been told to "go fish" and you pick a card of the rank you just asked for, you show the card immediately before putting it in your hand, and your turn continues. (In some very strict games, your turn would continue only if the card you fished for completed a book for you.)

When you get the fourth card of a book, you show all four, place them on the table in front of you, and continue your turn.

If a player is left without cards, she may draw from the stock at her turn and ask for cards of the same rank as the one she has drawn. After the stock has been used up, a player who has no cards is out of the game.

The game is over when all 13 books have been assembled. The player with the most books wins.

Tips

When a player asks for cards and gets them, but does not put down a completed book, you can tell that he has either two or three cards of that rank.

Suppose John requests Queens and gets one Queen from the player he has asked. John does not put down a book of Queens, but asks some new question and is told to "go fish." You now know that John held at least one Queen to give him the right to ask for Queens. He has received a Queen, which gives him a total of either two or three Queens.

In the same way, you know something else about a player's hand when he asks for a card and gets nothing at all. *For example, suppose John asks somebody for 8s and is told to go fish. You know that he must have at least one 8 in his hand.*

Little by little, you can build up information about the cards the other players are holding. If you know that another player has Queens, but you have no Queens yourself, the information does you no good. If you have a Queen yourself, however, you are then allowed to ask for Queens—and if you ask the right person because of the information you have, you may get as many as three Queens and be able to put down an entire book in front of you!

Hearts
OF PLAYERS: 2–6

This is the basic and most simple of the Hearts family, though not the most popular. It is almost always played with four people; if you have more players, other forms of the game are better.

You also need a handful of counters for this game, toothpicks, pebbles, dried beans, etc., the same number to each player—or paper and pencil.

The Object of the Game
To avoid winning any hearts—or to win all 13 of them.

The Deal

Each player receives 13 cards. When you can't divide them equally, remove enough 2s from the deck to make deal come out even. Aces rank highest.

The Play

The player to the left of the dealer makes an opening lead and the cards are played in tricks. A trick is won by the highest card played of the suit led. There is no trump suit, though Hearts are often mistakenly called trumps. The winner of a trick leads to the next trick.

Scoring with counters

For each Heart that a player wins, he must pay one counter into the pool.

If two or more players take no Hearts, they divide the pool. But if all the players take Hearts, nobody wins the pool. It stays on the table as a jackpot and becomes part of the pool for the next deal.

Scoring with paper and pencil

Each Heart taken counts one point against the player. A game can be ended at any agreed-upon time, and the player with the lowest total score is the winner. If a player wins all the Hearts, the usual method of scoring is to deduct 13 from his score. Some people deduct double that—26, instead.

King's Corner
OF PLAYERS: 2

The Object of the Game

To get rid of all the cards in your hand by playing them onto the layout.

The Deal

Remove the four Kings from the deck and lay them faceup to form four diagonal corners in a layout that will have four more faceup cards.

Deal four faceup cards, placing each between two Kings, to form the layout.

Deal eight cards to each player. Place the deck facedown in the middle of the table.

The Play

Players take turns. At each turn a player draws a card from the top of the deck and may play it onto the layout if it is opposite in color and one lower in value than one of the layout cards.

For example, you could play a red nine on a black ten, and a black Queen on a red King.

During her turn, a player may make all possible plays. If any of the cards in the layout itself can be placed on another, she may do it in her turn, filling the empty space with a card from her hand. Play continues until one player has no more cards and is the winner.

Klondike

OF PLAYERS: 1

This is probably the most popular solitaire game in the world.

The Layout

Lay out seven cards in a row facedown except for the first card. Then put the eighth card face up on the second card in the row, and complete the row with facedown cards. Place a faceup card on the third pile, and finish off the row in the same way. Continue until you have a faceup card on every pile. Your layout will look like the diagram on the next page.

The Object of the Game

Build up complete suits from Ace to King.

The Play

First, look over the spread carefully. Move any cards that you can to the foundation row—Aces and any cards you can build on them.

You can also build cards on the layout. Only faceup cards are available for building, and only if they are the exposed cards of the pile. Then you can build downwards on them in alternating colors.

In the example shown here you can move the Ace up to the foundation row, and then move the black 3 onto the red 4, and the red 2 onto the black 3.

Every time you move a faceup card, you turn up the facedown card beneath it. When there are no more facedown cards in a pile, you have a space. Spaces can be filled by any available King.

Put the Aces above the spread in the foundation row.

Square up the piles before you play.

When you've made all the moves you can, start going through the stockpile one by one, looking for more cards to build onto the foundations and the layout. If you can't place a card, it goes onto a wastepile, and the top card of the wastepile is available for play.

Scoring

Five rounds make a game. Add up the number of foundation cards you come up with in each round for your final score.

Linger Longer
OF PLAYERS: 4-6

The Object of the Game

To get all the cards and be the last player left when everyone else has dropped out. If two or more players are down to one card each at the end, the winner of the last trick wins the game. (A trick is a round in which each person plays a card according to certain rules; these are different, depending on the game.)

The Deal

Each player receives as many cards as there are players in the game. for example, with five players, each receives five cards.

The last card dealt, which goes to the dealer, is shown to all the players. It decides the trump suit for that trick. The rest of the deck is placed facedown in the middle of the table, forming the stock.

The Play

The player to the left of the dealer makes the first "lead" (play), putting down in the middle of the table any card in the trump suit, if he can. Otherwise, he can put down any card he pleases. The other players "follow suit," putting down any cards in their hand that are in the trump suit. Each player tries to capture the trick of four cards by playing the highest card of the suit that was led.

When a player wins a trick, he "owns" those cards. Then he draws the top card of the stock, which determines the trump suit for the next trick.

When a player is left without any cards, he has to drop out of the game, and the others play on.

Loo

OF PLAYERS: 5–8 (6 is best)

You need a handful of counters—toothpicks, pebbles, dried beans, etc. Give the same number to each player.

The Object of the Game

To win the most counters.

The Deal

Each player receives three cards, one at a time. An extra hand of three cards is dealt just to the left of the dealer. This is the "widow." If the player to the left of the widow does not like her hand, she may throw it away and take the widow instead. If she is satisfied with her hand, though, she must say so and stick with it.

Each player, in turn, has a chance to take the widow, until somebody takes it or all refuse it.

The Play (Single Pool)

After the matter of the widow is settled, the player to the left of the dealer makes the opening lead. You must always follow suit to the lead when you can. You must play a higher card than any other card in the trick, if you can. The highest card in the suit wins the trick. Aces are high.

Keep the tricks you have won faceup on the table in front of you as you play.

Trumps

The play begins without any trump suit and continues that way as long as everybody follows suit to every lead. When somebody fails to follow suit, the top card of the undealt stock is turned over. This card decides the trump suit. The trick that was just played is examined, and if a card that has been played turns out to be from the trump suit, that card wins the trick.

Scoring

To start a pool, the dealer must "ante up" three counters (put three of his counters in the middle of the table). When the pool contains no more than these three counters, it is a "single" and play takes place as before.

After the play, the pool pays out one counter for each

trick won. Players who have not won a trick must pay three counters into the next pool, making it a "double pool"—or jackpot.

Double Pool

This is formed by the dealer's ante of three counters plus any payments for "loo"— not winning a trick in the previous hand.

After the deal, the next card of the deck is turned up, deciding the trump suit. After checking out their hands, the players must say in turn whether they will play or drop out. If all but the dealer drop out, he takes the pool. If only one player ahead of the dealer decides to play, the dealer must play too. He may play for himself, in which case he may not take the widow, or he may play "to defend the pool," in which case he must throw away his hand and take the widow. When the dealer plays just to defend the pool, he neither collects nor pays any counters. The pool alone settles with his opponent.

The nearest active player to the left of the dealer leads first. The other rules of play are the same as in a single pool.

The double pool pays out one-third of its contents for each trick won. A player who stays in and does not win a trick, must pay three counters to the next pool.

Monte Carlo

OF PLAYERS: 1

The Layout

Deal five rows of five cards each, so your layout looks like the diagram on page 44:

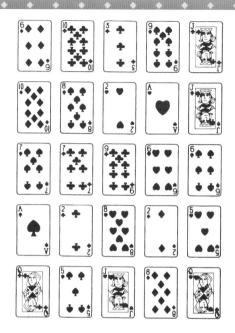

The Object of the Game

To discard the entire deck in pairs of the same rank. You can discard them if they are:

1. Next to each other
2. Above or below each other
3. "Touching" diagonally

The Play

Remove every pair that you can from the layout. When you do, there will be holes. Close up the cards so that all the holes are filled and the cards are in the same order in which you laid them out.

After you make the cards into solid rows again, deal

new cards to make up the bottom rows, so that you have five rows of five cards again.

Remove the pairs again in the same way, and when you can't move any more cards, close up the spaces in the layout again, and fill in again from the cards in your hand.

Napoleon
OF PLAYERS: 2-6

The Object of the Game
To correctly predict the number of tricks you will win in each round.

The Deal
Each player receives five cards, one at a time. Give out the counters, which may be poker chips, matchsticks, toothpicks, dried beans, etc., the same number to each player.

The Bidding
The player to the left of the dealer has the first turn. He "bids" (predicts) the number of tricks he will take if he is allowed to name the trump suit. Each player has one turn in which he may pass or may bid from one to five. A bid of five tricks is called "nap."

The Play
The highest bidder names the trump suit and makes the first lead, which must be a trump.

The cars are played in tricks. The players must follow suit to the lead card if they can. Otherwise, there is no restriction on what they may play or lead.

The winner of each trick leads to the new trick—playing any suit—and everyone continues to follow that lead. The trick is won by the highest card.

The bidder tries to win the number of tricks she has named. All the other players combine forces against her. Play stops the moment the outcome is sure—success or defeat for the bidder.

Scoring

When a bidder wins, she collects from each other player the same number of counters as her bid. If she is defeated, she plays this number to each player.

The bid of "nap" for all the tricks is special. If you make it, you collect ten counters from each player, but if you fail, you pay five to each one.

Old Maid

OF PLAYERS: 2 or more

The Object of the Game

To avoid getting "stuck" with the last unpaired Queen.

The Deal

Discard one Queen from the pack before beginning this game. Deal one card at a time to each player, as far as the cards will go. It doesn't matter if they don't come out even.

The Play

Sort your cards and put aside, facedown, all cards that

you can pair—two by two. For example, you might put aside two Kings, two Queens, two 7s, and so on. If you have three Queens and three Jacks, you would be allowed to put two of them aside, but the third card would stay in your hand.

After each player has discarded his paired cards, the dealer presents her cards, fanned out, but facedown, to the player at her left. The player at the left selects one card (blindly, since the hand is facedown) and quickly examines it to see if it pairs with some card still in his hand. If so, he discards the pair. In any case, this player now fans his cards out and presents them face down to the player at his left.

This game continues, each player in turn presenting his hand, fanned out and facedown, to the player to the left. Eventually, every card will be paired, except one of the Queens. The player who is left with the odd Queen at the end of the hand is the "Old Maid" or the "Odd One Out."

Whenever a player's last card is taken, he drops out. He can no longer be the "Old Maid" or the "Odd One Out."

Poker

 # OF PLAYERS: 4 or more

The Object of the Game
To have the highest-valued hand at the end of the game.

The Deal
Deal one card at a time until each player has five cards.

Value of the Cards and Hands

The cards are ranked from high to low with Aces always high and 2 as the lowest card. Some combinations of cards are considered better than others. Here is a list of the highest-valued hands, starting with the most valued.

Royal Flush: The Ace, King, Queen, Jack, and 10 all in a single suit.

Straight Flush: Any other uninterrupted sequence of cards in a single suit (such as the 4, 5, 6, 7, and 8 of hearts).

Four of a Kind: Four same-value cards plus one other card (such as four Kings and a 3).

Full House: Three same-value cards, plus any two other same-value cards (such as three Jacks and two 10s).

Flush: Five cards that all have the same suit (they do not have to be in order).

Straight: Five cards in an uninterrupted sequence that do not have to be of the same suit (such as a 2, 3, 4, 5, and 6 that are not all one suit).

Three of a Kind: Three same-value cards, plus any two other cards (if the other two cards are a pair, you have something better than Three of a Kind—a Full House).

Two Pair: Two same-value cards, plus two other same value cards, and any one other card (such as two 5s, two Queens, and a 10).

One Pair: Two same-value cards, plus any three other cards (if the other three cards are the same value as each other, you have the better hand called Full House).

High Card: If you do not have any of the other hands, whichever card you have with the highest value is your High Card (you would win if everyone else had this hand, but had a lower High Card).

The Play

First, each player places an ante or "token bet" into the pot (the middle of the playing area). You can use coins, poker chips, jelly beans, or anything you feel like using to bet with. This way, even if there is no more betting, the player with the highest-value hand will win something.

Then the dealer deals the cards face down around the table, starting at the player to his left and continuing clockwise. After each player has his or her five cards, the rest of the deck is placed in the middle of the table, and play begins.

Each player looks at his or her cards, and then the first player (the player to the left of the dealer) places a bet. In the next round, the person to her left will bet first, and so on until everyone has had a chance to bet first.

Players have several options as far as the first round of betting goes. If no one has made a bet yet, you have two choices:

Open: You may "open" the pot by making a bet. Generally, players bet higher when they have more highly valued hands, but this is not always the case—they might be trying to fool you!

Check: You may "check" by saying "Check." This means that you are not making a bet yet, but you will wait and see what is going to happen.

If and when someone opens the betting, you have three choices:

See: To "see" means to match the going bet. If someone has put in a nickel, or a jelly bean, or whatever counter you are using, you have to put in one of the same to keep playing the game.

Raise: To "raise" means to match the bet, and then add

something extra. If the player before you bet ten cents, you could "see" their ten cents and "raise" them another nickel. The new bet would be fifteen cents.

Fold: To "fold" means to put your cards face down on the table. This means giving up your chance to win, so if you think your hand is strong, you would probably not take this option. However, if the betting is high, and you only have High Card, you might want to "fold."

Now, everyone who is still playing (those who haven't folded) can discard the cards they don't want and replace them with new cards from the deck. This can help you to get a higher-valued hand. Each player chooses this option can discard one, two, or three cards and will receive an equal number of new cards from the deck. Both the discarded cards and the new cards are passed face down.

As soon as everyone who wants them has their new cards, a new round of betting starts. You have the same betting options as in the previous round (open or check; see, raise, or fold). The game is over when no player wants to raise, or all but one player have folded.

Now everyone who has not folded shows their cards. Whoever holds the highest-valued hand is the winner and takes all of the bets from the pot.

Strategy

If you think that you might have a good hand, try to stay in the game and get other players to drive the bets up. You don't want to bet extremely high too early and reveal that you might have a very good hand and cause everyone else to fold, but you also don't want to settle for small pot. Only fold when you think you absolutely must—the other players may be bluffing!

Tip

A good idea in poker is to maintain a neutral expression, known as a "poker face." That way, the other players will not know if you are excited about a good hand, disappointed by the trade-in, or if you are thinking that another player just bet way too high!

Pounce (Racing Demon)
OF PLAYERS: 2–8

This is a way of playing *Klondike* or *Canfield* as a round game.

The Object of the Game

To be the first player to get rid of all the cards onto the bases wins the game.

The Deal

Each player has his or her own deck. Each player lays out the cards for Klondike or Canfield—whatever game is chosen. Everybody must be given time to complete the layout. Then, at a signal, all begin to play.

The Play

Each plays the game in the usual way, building on his own piles, but all the base cards must be put in the middle of the table and they become everybody's property. A player may build on anybody's base cards.

If the play comes to a standstill before any of the players have gotten rid of all their cards, the base piles are sorted out and the cards are returned to their owners. The one who got the most cards onto the bases wins the game.

The game is very exciting, and the few rules need to be enforced strictly to keep it from getting rough. A player may put cards on the bases with one hand only—the right hand, if the person is right-handed. If several players try to put the same card on the same pile simultaneously, the one whose card is lowest wins the race and all the others must be taken back.

Quadrille
OF PLAYERS: 1

The Layout
You don't need to set up the layout for this game ahead of time, which is one of the great things about this game. You put the cards in place as they show up.

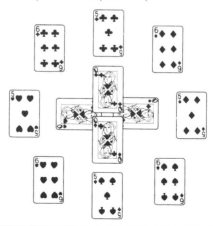

The Object of the Game

To build up the 6s in suit to the Jacks and the 5s down in suit to the Kings.

The Play

Start turning up cards from the deck. As soon as the 5s and 6s appear, put them in place and start building on them. On the 5s you build down: 4 3 2 Ace King.

On the 6s you build up: 7 8 9 10 Jack.

The queens just sit in the middle and look regal.

You get two re-deals (three times through the cards).

Rolling Stone

OF PLAYERS: 4–6

When four people play this game, use the Ace, King, Queen, Jack, 10, 9, 8, and 7 of each suit. If a fifth person plays, add 6s and 5s. If there is a sixth player, add the 4s and 3s. You need eight cards for each player.

The Object of the Game

To get rid of all your cards.

The Deal

Deal one card at a time until each player has eight cards. This uses up the pack.

The Play

The player to the dealer's left begins by putting down any card he pleases. Then the play moves to the left and the next player puts down another card in the same suit.

The turns continue, always moving to the left, with the other players following with another card of the same suit, if they can, playing high or low, as they please.

If all the cards in a suit are played, the person who put down the highest card leads again. And all the cards that were played to this first "trick" (sequence of cards) are turned over and put aside. For the purpose of winning a trick, the cards rank as follows:

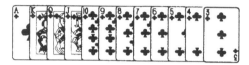

Highest   *Lowest*

When a player cannot put down a card of the same suit when it's her turn to play, she must pick up all the cards previously played in that sequence. This ends the trick. She then begins the next trick by leading with any card she chooses.

The process continues. In most games, a player picks up the cards several times. Eventually, one player will get rid of all his cards, and win the hand.

Scopa
OF PLAYERS: 2

This is an Italian game. Scopa means "broom."

The Object of the Game

The first player to get 11 points is the winner.

The Deal

Remove the 8s, 9s, and 10s from the deck.

The dealer deals four cards to each player and four faceup cards on the table.

Point Value of the Cards

All number cards equal their face value.

Jack = 8 points
Queen = 9 points
King = 10 points

The Play

Players take turns playing a card from their hands. A card may be used as a "match" to take in a card of the same value. Or it can take in more than one card, if the card to be played equals the total of two or more cards on the table.

For example, a 6 and a 2 on the table may be taken by a Jack (which is worth 8 points). A 3 and an Ace could be taken by a 4.

When you take in cards, keep them facedown in a pile in front of you.

If you manage at any point to pick up the last card on the table, that is a "scopa." Turn that card up in the pile of accumulated cards, to be scored separately when you tally your points.

After the four cards have been played out, the dealer deals four more to each player. The play continues until all the cards have been dealt. Then players tally their points.

Scoring

Each turned up card (scopa) = 1 point
Each seven = 1 point
King of Diamonds = 1 point
The most cards = 1 point
The most Diamonds = 1 point

Sevens

OF PLAYERS: 1

The Object of the Game

To get rid of all the cards.

Point Value of the Cards

Ace = 1
Jack = 11
Queen = 12
King = 13

The Play

Deal cards in a row, faceup. Remove all sevens and all cards that are next to each other that add up to seven or any multiple of seven.

For example, a King, worth 13, and an 8 side by side, add up to 21 [3 x 7] and therefore can be removed.

Shamrocks

OF PLAYERS: 1

Play the same way as "Clover Leaf" (see page 20) except:
1. If a King is on the top of a set and a card of lower rank in the same suit lies under it, you can put the King under that card.
2. No clover may contain more than three cards.

Snip, Snap, Snorem

OF PLAYERS: 3 or more

The Object of the Game
To get rid of all your cards.

The Deal
Deal one card at a time to each player, until the pack is used up. It doesn't matter if some players have more cards than the others.

The Play
The player to the left of the dealer puts any card faceup on the table. The next player to the left matches it with the same card in a different suit, saying "Snip."

The next player to the left matches the original card with the same card in a third suit, saying "Snap." The next player follows with the fourth card of the same kind, saying "Snorem." If a player is unable to follow with a matching card, he says "Pass," and his turn goes to the next player to the left.

Let's say that Allan puts down a 6 of Hearts. The next player to the left, Bette, has no 6 and therefore must say "Pass." Carol, the next player, has the 6 of Diamonds and puts it down, saying "Snip." Dennis, the player to the left, has both of the remaining 6s and puts them down one at a time, saying "Snap" for one and "Snorem" for the other.

Then Dennis (the player who said "Snorem,") after putting down the fourth card of a kind, plays the first card of the next group of four. If he has more than one of a kind, he must put down as many as he has instead of holding out one of the cards for "Snorem."

For example, if you decide to put down Kings, and you have two of them, you must put both of them down at the start. You're allowed to put down just one of them and wait for the other two Kings to appear before showing your remaining King for a "Snorem."

The first player to get of his cards wins the game.

Spit (Frenzy)
OF PLAYERS: 2

This double solitaire game, a version of "Spit," is played by two people. As you can tell from its name, it is a very fast game!

The Object of the Game

To be the first to get rid of all your cards.

The Deal

Deal two facedown piles of four cards each, one to the right of each player. These are the starter cards. Deal out the rest of the deck so that each player has a facedown pile. Players take the top four cards of their facedown piles as their "hand," replacing cards as they are played, so that each player always has a four-card hand.

The Play

Both players turn up the top card of the starter cards (to their right), placing the card faceup in the middle of the table, so that there are two cards side by side. These are the cards to be played upon.

Now, as fast as they can (no taking turns), the players try to play cards from their hands onto the faceup cards. A card may be played, regardless of suit, if it is one more or one less than the card on the table. So on a 7, you could play a 6 or an 8. On a King, you could play a Queen or an Ace. As plays are made, players take cards from their facedown pile, always keeping four cards in their hands.

When no more plays can be made, players again—at the same time—go to their starter cards, turn over the next card, put it into the middle of the table, and play resumes.

When the starter cards are used up, turn over the faceup playing cards in the middle of the table and use them to provide new starter cards.

Play continues until one player gets rid of all his cards and is the winner.

Spoof

 # OF PLAYERS: 2 or more

This game is also known as "Drop 7" and "Fan-Tan."

The Object of the Game
To get rid of all your cards.

The Deal
All the cards are dealt out.

The Play
Each player is allowed to play one card. The player to the dealer's right goes first, then each player in turn. To begin, the player must have the 7 of Diamonds, so the player has to pass if he cannot put down that card. The player who has it places it on the table.

Players in turn may play the 7 of Clubs or the 6 or 8 of Diamonds, placing the 6 on one side of the 7 and the 8 on the other side.

The next players may continue to place cards in sequence, building up (on the 8) or down (on the 6), or they may play a 7. But you can only play the suits in order. The 7 of Hearts may be played only after the 7 of Clubs has been played, and the 7 of Spades only after the 7 of Hearts.

Players must play a card if they have a play. Otherwise, they pass. Play continues until one player gets rid of all his cards and is the winner.

Tip
If you have a choice of plays, choose the one most likely to prevent your opponent from going out. For example, if

you suspect he has the Ace of Hearts, and you have the 2, you will hold it back so that he is unable to play that card.

War

The Object of the Game
To win all the cards.

The Deal
Deal one card to each player until the deck is divided in two.

The Play
The players put their stack of cards facedown in front of them and turn up the top card at the same time. The player who has the higher of the two turned-up cards wins both cards and puts them facedown at the bottom of his stack of cards. The King is the highest card, and the Ace is the lowest. The full rank of cards is:

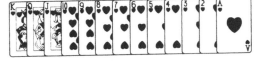

Sometimes "War" is played with the Ace high.

If the two turned-up cards are of the same rank, the players have a "war." Each turns one card facedown and one card faceup. The higher of the two new faceup cards takes both piles (a total of six cards).

If the newly turned-up cards again match, there is double war. Each player once again turns one card facedown and one card faceup, and the higher of these two new faceup cards wins the entire pile of ten cards.

The game continues until one player has all the cards.

This is a good game to play when you have a lot of time and nowhere to go.

Whist

OF PLAYERS: 4 in partnership

Whist is just about the simplest card game of all to play. What is not so simple is to play "Whist" well. The rules are simple and few. You can learn them in two minutes.

The Object of the Game

To win as many tricks as possible. Points for tricks and "honors" are accumulated, and the first side to reach a total of seven game points wins.

The Deal

Each player receives 13 cards, dealt one at a time. The last card of the pack, belonging to the dealer, is exposed to all the players. This card decides the trump suit for that hand.

The Rank

In every suit, the cards rank:

Highest 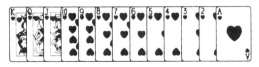 *Lowest*

The Play

The player to the left of the dealer makes the first lead. The hands are played out in tricks. You must follow suit to the lead, if you can. Otherwise, you may play or lead as you please. However, if a player revokes—by not following suit when he has in his hand an appropriate card to play—he and his partner have to pay a penalty. The penalty is decided upon before play begins, and may be as severe as two game points for the opponent. The partnership cannot win any trick in which it revokes.

A trick is won by the highest trump in it, or if it contains no trump, the highest card of the suit led. The winner of a trick makes the lead for the next trick.

One member of each partnership gathers together all the tricks won by his side. He doesn't throw them together in a single pile, but overlaps them crosswise, so that each batch of four cards remains separate from the others.

Scoring

The side that wins the majority of the tricks scores: 1 game point for each trick over six, and, if agreed upon, 2 game points should the opponents revoke.

In addition, points are scored for honors. The honors are the Ace, King, Queen, and Jack of the trump suit.

If 2 honors were dealt to each side, there is no score. If one side received 3 honors, it scores 2. For all 4 honors, the score is 4.

Remember that honors are scored by the side to which they are dealt, not won in play. Both sides may score in the same deal, one side winning a majority of tricks and the other side holding a majority of honors.

Index

GREAT CARD GAMES